SELF-SMART

Other Book by the Author

The Hidden Link Between Vision and Learning: Why Millions of Learning-Disabled Children Are Misdiagnosed (Rowman & Littlefield, 2016)

SELF-SMART

The Little Book with Big Ideas to Help Kids Thrive

Wendy Beth Rosen

ROWMAN & LITTLEFIELD
Lanham • Boulder • New York • London

Published by Rowman & Littlefield
A wholly owned subsidiary of The Rowman & Littlefield Publishing
Group, Inc.
4501 Forbes Boulevard, Suite 200, Lanham, Maryland 20706
www.rowman.com

Unit A, Whitacre Mews, 26-34 Stannary Street, London SE11 4AB

British Library Cataloguing in Publication Information Available

Library of Congress Cataloging-in-Publication Data Available

ISBN 978-1-4758-3306-5 (pbk : alk. paper)
ISBN 978-1-4758-3307-2 (electronic)

∞ ™ The paper used in this publication meets the minimum requirements
of American National Standard for Information Sciences Permanence of
Paper for Printed Library Materials, ANSI/NISO Z39.48-1992.

Printed in the United States of America

This book is for *you*.

With gratitude to my students, for being my teachers.
And with special thanks to Lauren Ariev Gellman,
for the opportunity.

CONTENTS

PREFACE

I imagine what drew you to read this book might well be the very same feelings that motivated me to write it. I first awakened to a sense that life seemed off-balance as a parent, when I noticed an unprecedented degree of pressure begin to envelop my children as they progressed through school. I tended to the strain of this with the empathetic heart of a mother, while trying to make sense of it with the experienced mind of a teacher.

Secretly, I was questioning our way of life as a species. When did the demands and expectations grow to feel so overwhelming and unmanageable? Frustrated but determined, I could only press on and try to help my kids manage in spite of their rising stress levels—and mine. I was also feeling increasingly resentful of how conditions were eroding our time together as a family.

My years of parenting, teaching, and nurturing in and out of the classroom have taught me what matters most. Conscious observance has driven home the understanding of what a developing human being needs in order to truly thrive. Children are the most precious, potential-laden treasures in our midst and need gentle, patient, and encouraging conditions in which to grow into the people they are meant to be.

Sadly, these ideal conditions can be hard to come by in our current way of life. Constant pressure and an endless barrage of demands are wearing us down and taking their toll. We are all caught up in it, but our kids attend school in what may be the most pressure-filled, stress-inducing environment since formal education began.

Children are vulnerable in this arduous era, and they need our time-tested perspective to help them navigate through it, while keeping their psyches intact so they can acquire the skills, attitudes, and behaviors that really count. As kids rise to full-fledged adulthood and we hand the future over to them, we want and need them to grow into caring, responsible, and compassionate individuals who possess the tools to become creative thinkers and valuable contributors to humanity.

In this current high-pressure academic culture, many kids are feeling powerless and overwhelmed. They may not even be aware of their own interests and special talents, simply because their to-do lists are endless, leaving them with little or no downtime to catch their breath and reflect. Instead, they may be *breathless* and grow disconnected from themselves.

If our children are going to have any chance to learn how to think, question, and become lifelong learners, it's going to take some creative leadership and attentive action. Beyond this lies the hope that they won't burn out on the way to figuring out who they are. Quite disturbingly, though, we are now seeing evidence of this imbalance catching up with them.

On college campuses across the country, unprecedented stress levels among students are resulting in an increase in mental health problems at alarming rates. College administrations are scrambling to pull together the support resources necessary to address the issue. Headlines and news reports about the crisis are materializing with greater frequency. Kiosks offering on-the-spot self-administering mental health questionnaires stand in student centers alongside ATMs and vending machines. We've entered a new era.

How did this happen? I'd argue that climate change is also occurring in schools, and kids are getting burned. We've brought the heat: Excessive pressure, overly rigorous expectations, and relentless workloads force kids to choose between grades or sleep, an unrelenting schedule or a healthy lifestyle, their future or the gift of being in the present moment during a pivotal time in their lives that they will never get back. It's time to ask the question, *What is their quality of life?*

We must focus our collective wisdom on bolstering our kids so they can withstand the precariousness of the times and emerge physically and mentally healthy and strong. Kids have the best shot at becoming confident, capable adults when they've got a team of experienced backers equipping them with the right tools and championing them on.

While this little booklet is geared toward high school students, its content is also relevant for college undergraduates who want to clarify their career goals and life path. It is filled with big ideas—the ones that make a difference, the ones that help us stay afloat and swim through the ever-changing currents of our lives. These are the tools that get us through when we are put to the test, but they are unfortunately shelved while we prep for all those other tests, the ones that ultimately won't make our kids smarter.

We know that educating our kids is a team effort and takes a dedicated, dynamic partnership between families and schools. Within these pages are essential values and tools that can make us all not only strong but also *well*, minus the cultural clutter that can muddy the waters and confound the journey. Simple, practical activities are presented to provide you with concrete methods to guide kids on the way to figuring out what their strengths are and what makes them unique.

It's worthwhile to take a moment here to mention what this book is not about, which are some other very important tools that successful learners need in school and throughout life. These include:

- Effective listening
- Active reading
- Selective reading
- Effective note-taking
- Strategic test prep and test-taking
- Resourcefulness

- Research skills
- Writing skills

There are already many wonderful books in existence about these skills that can help fill in the gaps where support is needed. You can find some of them listed in the "References" section at the end of this booklet. This conspectus you are holding is about cultivating greater self-awareness, which will help kids learn to recognize any of these skills that either don't come naturally to them or that they weren't taught. This is an important step in knowing which measures we can take to help shore them up.

Ultimately, we want to help our kids to find their own way and to find themselves. This specialized compass will guide you in helping them accomplish this by clarifying priorities and defining values. Its substance is succinct, timeless, and essential.

After reading this guidebook, you will be prepared to help the kids in your world:

- **Identify their own special set of strengths and abilities**
- **Explore what makes them unique**
- **Contemplate what their goals are for their future**
- **Chart a personal course of action to reach those goals and kick off the rest of their lives**

ACKNOWLEDGMENTS

When I was asked to teach a study skills class for high school students, I had no idea that I would become the student as much as the teacher. I devised a curriculum and hit the ground running. I soon found myself wishing I'd had the opportunity to acquire this knowledge in high school myself and only hoped my students were learning as much as I was! Once I understood the importance of self-knowledge in the learning process, the idea to distill the essence of this insight into a concise, handy guidebook sprang forth.

To the entire team at Rowman & Littlefield, I cannot tell you enough how lovely an experience it has been to work with all of you. To Dr. Tom Koerner—I extend my deep gratitude for your vision and belief in this work. Your support and guidance have been invaluable, and I feel privileged to have worked with you. To Carlie Wall—I offer my deepest thanks for your advice, accessibility, and assurance. You provided me with constant sustenance, and I appreciate this very much. To Kellie Hagan—I share my thanks and appreciation for your talents in shaping this manuscript into a unique and engaging creation. I'm so glad to have had the opportunity to collaborate with you.

I am fortunate to have in my midst a multitalented, interdisciplinary array of extraordinary colleagues who have provided insight and feedback to this project throughout its development. My warmest thanks and heartfelt appreciation go out to Lauren Ariev Gellman, Elizabeth Asamoah, Dr. Maurice Elias, Jackie Haines, Chip Wood, Jordan Siegel, Dr. Jeffrey Kress, Ruth Margolin, Rob Schweitzer, Terry Chazan Rothberg, Ildiko Henni-Jones, Marshal Datkowitz, and Wendy Hurwitz-Kushner.

And to my wonderful family—thank you, Mitchel, Sara, and Jonah, for providing me with laughter and love.

Part One

Unique Intelligences

METACOGNITION

A Key to Success

"I cannot teach anybody anything. I can only make them think."—Socrates

How can we ensure that the learning process unfolds successfully for our kids in an educational system and in a world that are growing more unsustainable in so many ways? The concept of sustainability permeates every area of our lives. In addition to encompassing the very basic "outer" needs for living—food, clothing, and shelter—there are other less-discussed, essential "inner" needs that are of great importance.

Basic needs enable us to live in the most primal sense; we need these three outer ingredients for survival. But if we want to thrive, then we must acknowledge and attend to our "inner" emotional, social, and psychological needs. The need for love, acceptance, security, and belonging must be recognized so that we can feel purposeful and whole.

As high school students and young adults, kids naturally have a lot on their minds. Being a student is their occupation in life. Yet, how often do we ask our kids how that's going? Grades, homework assignments, and tests aside, how do they feel about school, learning, and this full-time job of theirs? Beyond the academics and extracurriculars that they slalom through each day, their inner landscapes are experiencing profound change and growth. Having the chance to contemplate who they are becoming, where they are in their lives, where they wish to go, and how they will get there is a necessary and worthwhile endeavor, but unfortunately, it is not given enough priority. It is challenging these days for kids to hit the pause button and just have time to breathe and practice self-care.

Our collective consciousness is now acknowledging the importance of giving time and attention to ourselves and that doing so is not being selfish. As intuitive as it should seem, we've needed to culturally awaken to the notion that this is vital for our well-being. In the midst of juggling the many roles and responsibilities we have in our lives, taking care of ourselves is not only an essential act of kindness but also necessary if we wish to flourish. Kids need to learn the value of this, too.

This is where we come in. While the foundations on which they'll build the rest of their lives are being constructed, we need to teach our kids that it's not just about grades and scores. It's also about growing up to live a healthy, balanced life. And, in order to do this, one must become a lifelong learner. Lessons for living are everywhere along our paths through our everyday lives. We must be open to the opportunities to learn from everything and everyone. This is how we grow, and if we do not grow, then we become stagnant or, worse, we atrophy.

Kids who understand the value of learning not only will make the best students in school but also will have a greater chance of finding success, happiness, and fulfillment throughout their lives. Through the area of study in education referred to as *metacognition* ("learning how one learns" or having an "awareness or analysis of one's own learning or thinking processes"), a lot of research has resulted in a greater understanding among educators about *how* we learn.

We all have our own impressions about how intelligent we think we are. We often say to ourselves, "I'm good at _____." or "I'm not good at _____." One of the ideas about human intelligence that has received much attention over the last thirty years, the multiple intel-ligences theory, proposes that there are actually many different ways in which intelligence can express itself.

MULTIPLE INTELLIGENCES

Finding Strength and Direction

"Everybody is a genius. But if you judge a fish by its ability to climb a tree, it will live its whole life believing that it is stupid."—Unknown

Dr. Howard Gardner of Harvard University has spent a great deal of his career researching how we learn and is considered the father of the theory of multiple intelligences. The following is a list of all eight intelligences based on his research findings, with their corresponding characteristics. We all possess a combination of these intelligences to varying degrees. Some present themselves as great strengths, and others express themselves less significantly.

As you read through the lists, you may even become aware of a new perspective about yourself—strengths and interests that you didn't realize you had. Though you no doubt know yourself well, this is an exercise that we can take part in at any stage of life, which can provide exciting new insights about ourselves as we continue to grow. You may even find that your unique blend of intelligences overlaps with your areas of interest because we often have fun doing what we're good at. Helping kids identify their strengths is a meaningful way that we can help them learn about themselves.

Print out these lists, make them into wall charts for your classroom, or utilize them in whichever creative ways you feel would enable your kids to explore their inventories, make connections between themselves and the vast pool of strengths, and reflect on their unique abilities and talents.

VERBAL/LINGUISTIC INTELLIGENCE: "WORD SMART"

Learners with this strength:

- Think in words
- Use spoken and written language effectively to express themselves
- Understand the order and meaning of words
- Remember words and their definitions easily
- Use language to express and appreciate complex meanings

LOGICAL/MATHEMATICAL INTELLIGENCE: "NUMBER/REASONING SMART"

Learners with this strength:

- Analyze problems logically
- Calculate and carry out mathematical operations
- Excel at complex mathematical calculations
- Recognize and understand abstract patterns
- Perceive relationships and connections
- Use abstract, symbolic thought and deductive reasoning

VISUAL/SPATIAL INTELLIGENCE: "PICTURE SMART"

Learners with this strength:

- Think in three dimensions
- Recognize, use, and interpret images and patterns
- Reproduce objects in three dimensions
- Understand and recognize relationships between objects
- Possess a strong imagination

MUSICAL INTELLIGENCE: "MUSIC SMART"

Learners with this strength:

- Perform, compose, and appreciate musical patterns
- Understand the structure of music naturally
- Attune themselves to sounds and rhythms
- Recognize changes in pitch, tone, rhythm, and timbre
- Apply mathematical thinking patterns to music, which often overlap

BODILY/KINESTHETIC INTELLIGENCE: "BODY SMART"

Learners with this strength:

- Use the body for expression
- Manipulate objects and use a variety of physical skills
- Expertly control movement and coordination (fine motor, gross motor, or both)
- Naturally incorporate a sense of timing
- Find it easy to connect the mind with the body

NATURALIST INTELLIGENCE: "NATURE SMART"

Learners with this strength:

- Recognize and appreciate relationships in the natural world
- Discriminate among living things (plants and animals)
- Are sensitive to features of the natural world
- Possess a deep understanding and respect for nature

INTERPERSONAL INTELLIGENCE: "PEOPLE SMART"

Learners with this strength:

- See things from the perspectives of others easily
- Communicate well verbally and nonverbally
- Work well with others
- Understand people's intentions, motivations, and desires
- Are sensitive to the moods and temperaments of others
- Create and maintain healthy relationships

INTRAPERSONAL INTELLIGENCE: "SELF-SMART"

Learners with this strength:

- Understand themselves
- Understand their "self" in relation to others
- Are aware and capable of expressing their feelings
- Interpret and appreciate their own thoughts and motivations and use this knowledge in planning their lives
- Appreciate the *self* and the human condition

INTELLIGENT STRATEGIES FOR THE WIN IN SCHOOL AND IN LIFE

"If we did all the things we are capable of, we would literally astound ourselves."—Thomas Edison

Once we know our unique set of strengths, we can use this information to help us in many ways and in all kinds of situations. What is especially important for kids to realize is that they can use this knowledge to help them find the best practices for becoming successful learners. If they already consider themselves successful learners, then this will help them "up their game" even more. Why is this important?

From early on in school, kids are told to "study" for tests and do any number of assignments that involve skills they were likely never taught. There are methods for studying, and there is a science to learning, but strangely enough, this information is rarely discussed or even taught in school, even though it holds the underpinnings of everything students *do* in school.

Self-knowledge is powerful, but the truth is, often students are self-taught in this area. Left up to their own inner resources and outer variable circumstances, the chances for success vary greatly, despite the uniform model of education we attempt to provide.

The more we can build *metacognitive fitness* in our kids, the greater their capacity for learning and success. Just as parents must accept that their children will seek out others to serve as additional role models to learn from, so, too, must we realize that there is no way anyone is going to pick up all the knowledge and information needed while in school. We want our kids to be able to *learn how to learn* and appreciate that learning is an ongoing, life-enhancing, regenerating practice.

The following is a list of effective study strategies that students can put into play based wholly on their unique set of intelligences. This will help them build a strong foundation on which to nurture productive future study habits. These specific techniques symbiotically align with the characteristics intrinsic to each intelligence type. Learners can combine any number of them depending on what feels right to them. Being creative and personalizing this is *key*. Encouraging kids to take ownership of this exercise will help them become proactive learners for life.

STUDY STRATEGIES FOR INTELLIGENCE TYPE

Verbal/Linguistic Intelligence

- Read alone, but review with a partner or group
- Create flash cards
- Rewrite or outline basic ideas and information
- Highlight (no more than 10 percent of text)
- Write mnemonics

Logical/Mathematical Intelligence

- Create charts and graphs
- Find patterns in information
- Outline information in a logical progression
- Mix up study locations and styles (e.g., alone or in groups)

Visual/Spatial Intelligence

- Post important points and images on the walls of your study area
- Make colorful drawings, maps, or graphs (literal or metaphorical) of key concepts
- Use visualization when studying
- Keep your study area neat, clutter-free, and well-organized to minimize distraction

Musical Intelligence

- Read your notes into a digital recorder and play them back while you are in the car, working out, and so on
- Play music while studying
- Explain study concepts aloud to study buddies
- Create rhymes and songs out of words for study material; put information to beats or rhythms
- Take a music break when studying

Bodily/Kinesthetic Intelligence

- Type out your notes as you read
- Walk around while studying (watch out for obstacles!)
- Keep your hands busy with a stress ball, yo-yo, or other small object while you read or study
- Take frequent breaks to stretch and move your body

Naturalist Intelligence

- Study in a natural setting or with individuals or groups with similar interests
- Take breaks to connect with nature when studying
- Play "nature sounds" music in the background while studying
- Keep a beautiful plant in your workspace

- Sip healthy herbal tea to nourish your body and spirit

Interpersonal Intelligence

- Study with people
- Teach others the information you are learning
- Discuss information in order to retain it
- Take social breaks between study sessions or topics (reviewing the material with a friend or family member during your break is a good idea.)
- Take on group projects or interview assignments when possible

Intrapersonal Intelligence

- Create a quiet, cozy, comfortable workspace
- Keep separate, attractive journals for each subject
- Reflect on the personal meaning of ideas (what does it all mean to me?)
- Surround yourself with meaningful mementos that inspire you

* * *

Source: Michael Geisen, *The Great Courses: How to Become a SuperStar Student*. Chantilly, VA: The Great Courses, 2011. DVD.

Part Two

Traits for Success

INTERNAL SKILLS AND EXTERNAL SKILLS

The Ins and Outs of Victory

"With self-discipline most anything is possible."—Theodore Roosevelt

Think of someone you know personally who inspired you. They may be living or no longer living. Why did they inspire you? What character traits did they have that you feel factor into why you consider them an inspiration? What do you admire about them?

The following is an excerpt from a story in *Sports Illustrated* that is not only inspiring but also truly amazing:

> [Evelyn] Tripp, a 95-year-old grandmother of nine, was named USA Track and Field's masters long distance runner of the year in the women's 90-and-up age group for the fourth straight time. Tripp, who took up walking as rehab at 82 after she was injured in a car accident and then progressed to running, set a pending national 5K record for women 95-and-over with a time of 48:45 at the Reedy River Run in Greenville, S.C., in March. She holds the state 5K records for women ages 85–89, 90–94 and 95–99. (*Sports Illustrated*, January 9, 2012)

Which character traits do you think *she* has? Evelyn Tripp's incredible achievements are the results that the rest of the world sees. What we don't see is what went on inside Evelyn that enabled her to bounce back from adversity and achieve what she did. What's even more compelling is that she accomplished such amazing feats at a time in her life when, sadly, many see this as a period of decline and degeneration. Evelyn must have had remarkable inner strength, resolve, and belief in her own potential that served as a guiding force in her recovery and *regeneration*. Evelyn's story beautifully illustrates two types of skills I refer to as external skills and internal skills.

External skills are those actions and behaviors that are visible to others and are based on what we do outwardly in our lives and in the world. *Internal skills* are those attributes we possess inside ourselves that enable us to do what we do in our lives and in the world. We might also think of these as character traits. These two skill sets are central to success in life. There are specific traits that great students share that employ both types and that enable them to thrive.

CHARACTERISTICS OF GREAT STUDENTS: SETTING GOALS, GETTING ORGANIZED, FINDING BALANCE

First, great students *set goals* for themselves. These guide their decisions about how to spend their time and energy. To strive for a balanced life, kids should try to set at least one goal in each of these six areas:

1. Academic grades
2. Social life
3. Sports and exercise
4. Family and community
5. Hobbies and interests
6. Long-term plans

Great students are also *organized*. They won't always figure this out on their own, so it's our job to help them learn the value of organization. It's important for them to get a handle on how to organize their stuff, their time, and their brains. Kids need to have space for themselves where they will not be distracted, as well as a place for their work, folders, files, notebooks, journals, backpacks, and everything else they need. Kids should learn that using a weekly planner or agenda is a practice that begins in school but should also become a regular part of their lives going forward, as they take on more responsibility and need to keep track of their to-do lists. We can help kids understand the importance of scheduling their time so that they can devote attention to other things in their lives besides school, while meeting their basic needs and striving for balance.

Note: Electronics are a time sucker! Suggesting that they turn off all electronics not needed for assignments may be like asking them to fork over a limb, but developing self-discipline and resolving to check e-mail or texts only after they have finished their work will go a long way in helping them create good techno-hygiene habits. (If this is too hard, then they can give themselves a five-minute break every half hour to "check in," setting a timer so they don't get lost in cyberspace.) This is going to take real effort, as we know, because this is something we need to pay attention to, as well. It could go a long way, though, in coaching kids through it if we own up from the start and also commit to working toward this goal for ourselves.

It's helpful to acknowledge straight out that obligations kids don't typically enjoy or are not of their choosing, like homework, have a tendency to expand like a gas and fill up whatever amount of time is available. They can remedy this by learning to create boundaries that enable them to responsibly focus their attention on what needs to get done, so they can maintain their sanity and have time for activities that their own hearts desire.

And while we're on the subject, let's debunk the myth of multitasking. Growing bodies of scientific research indicate that there is no such thing as multitasking; we're just switching our attention among several different tasks, and the result is twofold:

- No one task is getting the full attention it deserves and needs in order to be done well.
- The "better" you think you are at multitasking (that is, the more you *think* you can do at once), the worse you are at everything you're doing.

Finally clueing into this, our collective culture has coined the term *uni-tasking*, a fresh, modern expression for the age-old practice of "doing one thing at a time." We can help kids (and ourselves) undo the practice of multitasking that has become the norm by teaching and modeling how to be fully present, how to tune into the needs and wishes of the moment at hand, and how to follow up with attitudes and actions that are energizing, motivating, and productive.

Great students *lead balanced lives*. Kids feel balanced when they are meeting their goals, feeling a sense of fulfillment, and having fun. Balance does not come about by itself. It takes effort. It needs to be given attention and managed with intention.

Great students are *curious*. This is what being a student is all about. Unfortunately, all too often, kids refrain from asking questions because they fear being judged or laughed at. It is crucial that we provide safe spaces in which students learn that *asking questions is actually one of the smartest things they can do.*

Sit down with the kids in your life, and talk about these characteristics. Prompt them to think about their short-term and long-term goals. Give them the logistic and emotional support they need to get and stay organized. Share why it is important to strive for balance, and divulge your efforts to achieve this in your own life. We are all a work in progress. Acknowledge the challenges, and brainstorm solutions and strategies. Interpersonal dialogue is one of the best ways to connect and enable kids to feel seen, heard, and validated. Actualizing their developing ideas is an inside job in the end, and this will only occur if they are able to mold, strengthen, and apply their internal skill sets. Encouragement and guidance from you will give them confidence and purpose.

* * *

Source: Michael Geisen, *The Great Courses: How to Become a SuperStar Student*. Chantilly, VA: The Great Courses, 2011. DVD.

INTERNAL SKILLS INVENTORY

Taking Stock, Taking Charge

"Optimism is the faith that leads to achievement. Nothing can be done without hope and confidence."—Helen Keller

What follow are twelve essential internal skills, which are the force behind just about everything we do that is worthwhile. We all need these skills and the qualities they are comprised of. We all learn them either directly or indirectly over the course of growing up, and we all continue to relearn them as we go through life. It is imperative that we teach and model these attributes to kids:

- Positive attitude
- Confidence
- Inspiration
- Perseverance
- Caring
- Responsibility
- Initiative
- Motivation
- Problem-solving
- Teamwork

- Effort
- Self-discipline

A word must be mentioned here on the importance of a positive attitude. It is taught by wilderness experts that, if one finds himself or herself in a survival situation, then a positive attitude may be the most essential tool that can influence the outcome of the situation. It is at the top of the priority list, followed by first aid, shelter, fire, water, and food, in that order. It is that important, and if it can make such a difference in a survival situation, then think how much difference it can make under everyday circumstances.

So, how can our kids learn to use this new self-knowledge in meaningful ways, so that they understand its value and feel its influence? They need a plan.

* * *

Source: Dorothy Rich, *MegaSkills: In School and in Life—The Best Gift You Can Give Your Child*. Boston: Houghton Mifflin, 1992.

THE SELF-ACTUALIZATION THESIS

An Action Plan for Life

"This moment deserves your full attention, for it will not pass your way again."—Dan Millman

Meet the SaT, not the SAT (the standardized test). The new version is the SaT: a *Self-actualization Thesis*. There is a big difference! This is what colleges should require for admission. Such a tool would tell an admissions team so much more about a student, about the person behind the grades and the scores.

Presented here is a culminating exercise that creates an opportunity for kids to reflect on how well they know themselves at this point in their lives and to pull together all the intrapersonal knowledge you are helping them glean. They can use this knowledge to design an action plan, or a map for their life, that can help them find their way as they get ready to venture out into the world and start to build their own lives.

They have begun to identify their unique set of strengths, intelligences, and interests. They have learned about *internal skills* and *external skills*, the character traits shared by successful learners, and the importance of goal setting. It's now up to them to chart a course of action based on where they've been, where they are now, and where they want to go.

Following are questions for reflection that draw on the points explored in this booklet. Kids can reflect on these independently, with your guidance, or both. Once they have given these essential questions thought and attention, they'll be ready to take things to a whole new level.

ACTION PLAN QUESTIONS

1. What are your unique strengths, interests, and abilities?
2. Which personal goals and aspirations, both large and small, would you like to set for yourself?
3. Which internal skills do you possess? Which do you want to acquire or strengthen?
4. What are some external skills you have demonstrated? Which achievements would you like to realize?

Help them carve out space and time to brainstorm; get creative; and find a way to "map" their strengths and interests, internal and external skills, and goals into a unique representation of themselves—their own personal SaT. This is like no other project they have ever taken on. It is an evolving portrayal of their unique, individual *selves.*

They can choose to identify this effort by any name that represents what it is and will become for them. This is a very powerful exercise and one that they can revisit on their own at any time. They are not being graded on this, and they will not be turning this in to anyone. They are the only person who will see it, unless they choose to share it with others. Therefore, they are the only person they're accountable to for it, which in and of itself embodies the ultimate lesson of this activity—they are, when all is said and done, accountable to themselves.

The effort kids put into this can support them throughout the rest of their lives because they are committing themselves to developing habits and mind-sets that are very powerful. This is a tool they may refer to any time they need to revisit any aspect of themselves or their lives, to clarify their goals, to refocus their efforts, or to make changes. Kids should consider this creation a cherished new possession, a prized personal heirloom, a master work. Help them run with it!

What follow are possible formats kids can utilize for this exercise that also tap into the multiple intelligences. They can choose from this list or think of their own ideas. Ideally, we want them to find the means of expression that work for them. This is not an assignment. It should not feel like work. Rather, if they follow their inner voice, they will feel energized, inspired, excited, and invested in this project that is *all about them*. Kids are the authors of their own life stories; teach them to *own* their life stories!

SELF-ACTUALIZATION THESIS PROJECT OPTIONS

Verbal/Linguistic Intelligence

- Journal
- Poetry
- Creative writing
- Word collage
- Storyboard
- Letter
- Calendar
- Autobiography
- Essay
- Storytelling
- Portfolio

Logical/Mathematical Intelligence

- Chart

- Graph
- Computer program
- Graphic organizer
- Flowchart
- Outline
- Time line
- Calendar
- Web
- Time sequence chart
- Story grid
- T-chart

Visual/Spatial Intelligence

- Drawing
- Model
- Chart
- Collage
- Graph
- Poster
- Video project
- Checklist
- Diagram
- Portfolio
- Map
- Montage
- Experiment
- Computer graphic
- Illustration
- Photography
- Scrapbook

Musical Intelligence

- Song

- Rap
- Music and video production
- Musical composition
- Rhythmic poetry
- Music performance

Bodily/Kinesthetic Intelligence

- Physical exercise routine
- Dance
- Work folder
- Checklist
- Collection
- Experiment
- Game
- Invention
- Project
- Sport

Naturalist Intelligence

- Nature imagery (photos, CDs, collections)
- Experiment
- Nature walk
- Outdoor activity
- Reading about, writing about, drawing, and photographing nature
- Caring for plants and animals
- Drawing inspiration from observation in nature

Interpersonal Intelligence

- Discussion
- Role-play
- Checklist

- Personal project poster
- Interview
- Peer coaching

Intrapersonal Intelligence

- Diary
- Journal
- Autobiography
- Guided imagery
- Photo essay
- Portfolio
- Independent contract
- Personal project poster
- Metacognitive survey
- Questionnaire

> "Find out who you are, and be that person. That's what your soul was put on this earth to be. Find that truth, live that truth, and everything else will come."—Ellen DeGeneres

* * *

Source: Sandra Schurr and Imogene Forte, *Curriculum and Project Planner for Integrating Learning Styles, Thinking Skills, and Authentic Instruction*. Nashville, TN: Incentive Publications, Inc., 2003.

AFTERWORD

Crafting a Built-in GPS

Kids take a driver's education class in school and work toward earning the privilege of maneuvering a high-powered vehicle through the world. We know fully well that driving is a privilege, not a right, and as such needs to be earned and upheld. This is driving in the literal sense.

However, we also need to help kids think about themselves as drivers in the metaphorical sense. This book is a decidedly different "driver's ed" manual of sorts. It can help them learn how to maneuver themselves through the world, highlighting another truth we also know fully well: They, too, are high-powered vehicles!

We want them to be in the driver's seat of their own lives, and it's important to help them get a firm grip on the steering wheel with both hands and to teach them to keep their eyes on the road ahead of them. Above all, we want them to have a reliable GPS, their own *Great Personal Sense*. This book is intended to help them develop it and use it to navigate their way through their lives. Listed in the "References" section are websites that offer a wealth of resources for further exploration that will complement the work you begin here with *Self-Smart*, including practical tools, like self-assessment surveys, supplementary links, and articles on the latest research in metacognition. There's a vast amount of top-notch information that is readily accessible and that will further illuminate this juncture that is just the beginning of lifelong learning, discovery, and infinite possibilities.

Let's help them have a great journey!

A SPECIAL NOTE TO KIDS

You are a very lucky kid. Not only do you have many strengths and abilities and talents and interests and wonderful personality traits, but you also have some special adults in your life who are watching out for you. You are reading this because they have been thinking about you a lot and reflecting on how they can help you become your best self.

It is so very important for you to discover what and how you think and feel about the world and everything in it. When you are able to do this as you travel through life, you will always be at home with yourself. This is a key that will help you open the many doors you will go through.

Know, most of all, that you are full of goodness and potential. Your success is in your own hands. You're becoming equipped now with important skills and self-knowledge. Every moment of every day offers you a choice. You need only to believe in yourself, now and always.

REFERENCES

BOOKS

The Everything Study Book (Fort Collins, CO: Adams Media, 1997) by Steven Frank

Multiple Intelligences: The Theory in Practice: A Reader (New York: Basic Books, 1993) by Howard Gardner

Study Smart, Study Less: Earn Better Grades and Higher Test Scores, Learn Study Habits That Get Fast Results, and Discover Your Study Persona (New York: Ten Speed Price, 2011) by Anne Crossman

WEBSITES

Habits of Mind, http://habitsofmind.org

MIDAS Profile, http://www.miresearch.org

MI Oasis, http://multipleintelligencesoasis.org

Study Guides and Strategies, http://www.studygs.net/index.htm